SCRIBBLE · COLOUR · CREATE
For Hours of Doodle Fun

SCRIBBLE DOODLES!

Crazy Creatures!

Illustrated by Lauren Nickless, Matt Ward,
Simon Abbott and Tim Charnick.

Draw a Dalmatian among the spots.

What's in the Secret Garden?

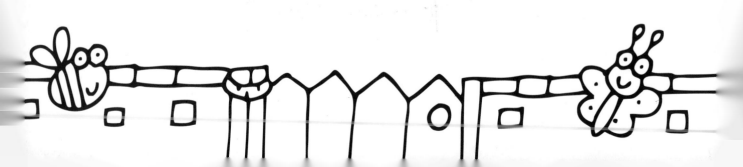

Fill the rock pool with creatures you'd expect to Find here.

Close your eyes and doodle a dog with a juicy bone.

Draw as many things as you can
think of that are green.

DRAW a SHipWreck at the bottoM
OF tHiS oceaN SceNe.

DRAW SOME SEA CREATURES IN THE SEA.

DRAW THE CREATURES
THAT LIVE IN
THESE SHELLS.

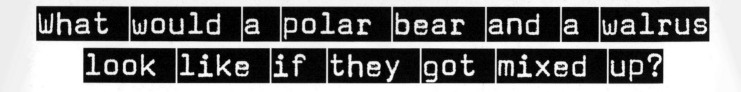

What would a polar bear and a walrus look like if they got mixed up?

**Use torn up
pieces of a magazine
to create a spring scene.**

DRAW SOME ANIMALS ON THIS FARM.
DON'T FORGET THE FARMER!

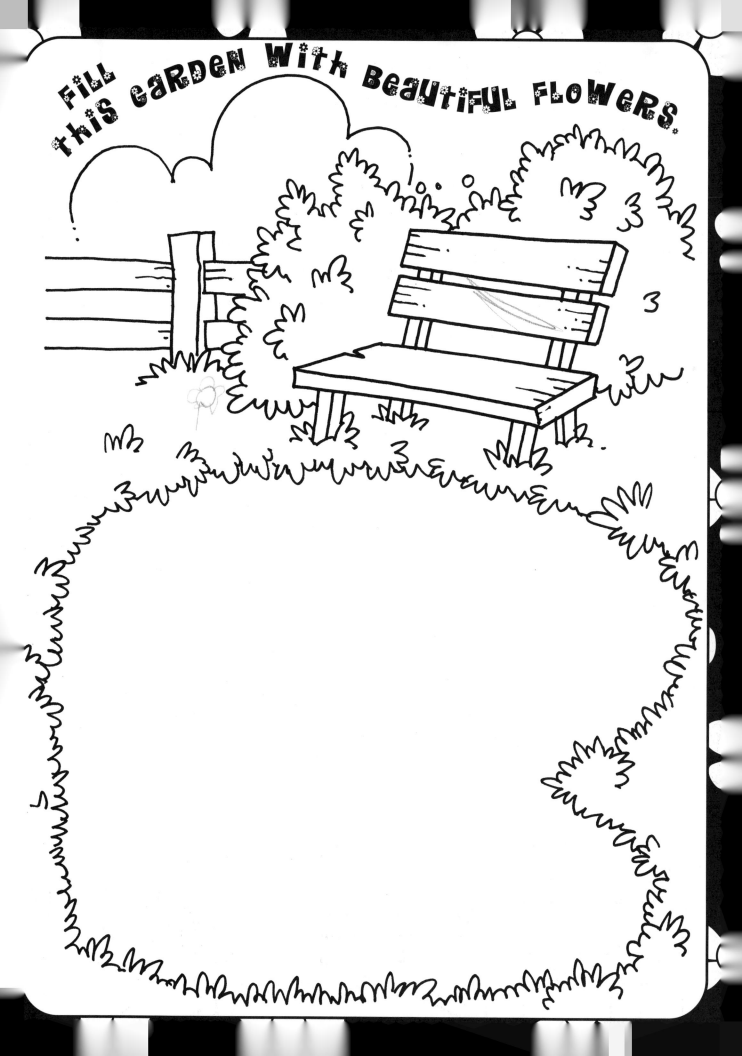

Fill this garden with beautiful flowers.

DRAW DIFFERENT TYPES OF FRUIT
ON THESE TREES.

Cut out pictures of things you like from old magazines and newspapers and create a garden collage.

CUCKOO!

IT'S SPRINGTIME!
DRAW SOME MORE CHICKS.

FILL THIS GARDEN WITH AS MANY INSECTS AS YOU CAN THINK OF.

Who is swinging from the jungle vine?

Give this dolphin a pod to swim with.

FIND THE SEAHORSES AMONG THE SEAWEED. DRAW SOME MORE.

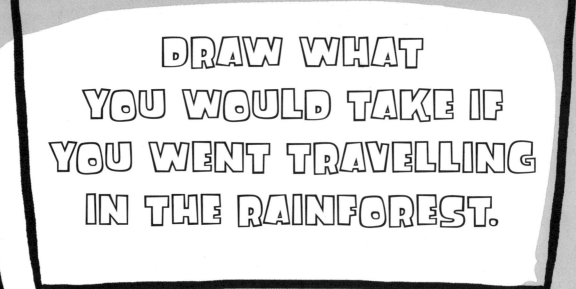

DRAW WHAT YOU WOULD TAKE IF YOU WENT TRAVELLING IN THE RAINFOREST.

Draw a picture of a rabbit without lifting your pencil from the paper.

Imagine you are an explorer.
What would you look like?

YOU HAVE DISCOVERED
A NEW TYPE OF BIRD.
DRAW IT IN THE TREE.

HOW MANY THINGS CAN YOU THINK OF THAT BEGIN WITH THE LETTER D? DRAW THEM.

Trace around your hand and use your imagination to create a wacky picture or pattern.

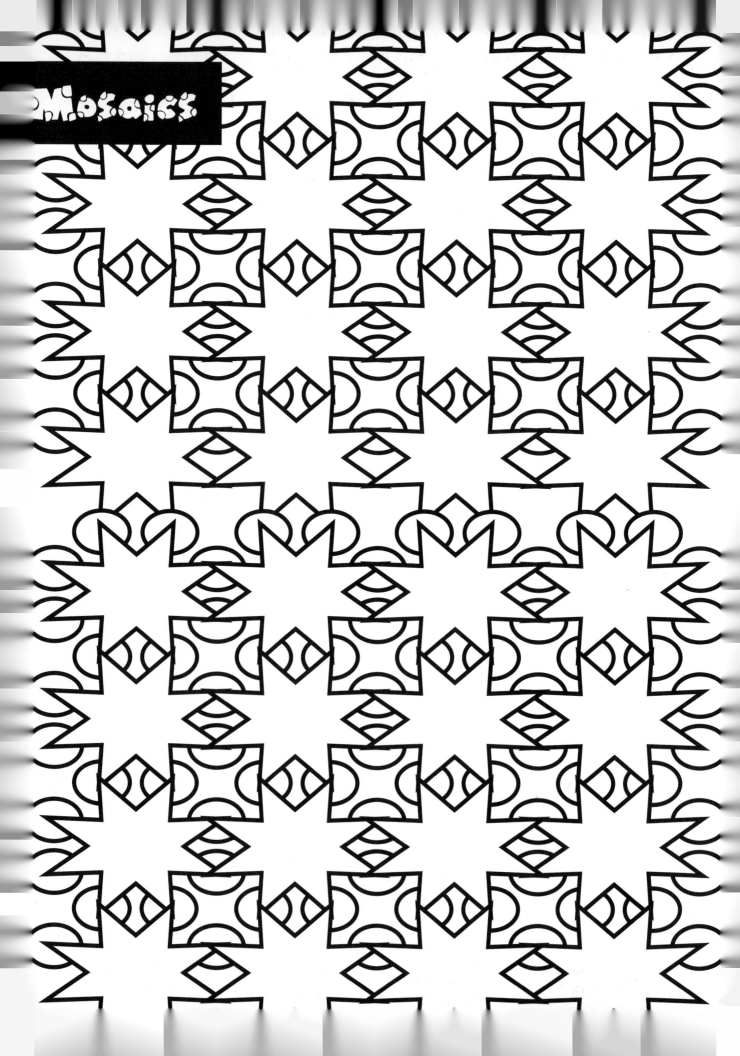

Mosaics

Design a newspaper front cover with the story that you've just become a celebrity.

Our artist has drawn
a combination of a
fish, a monkey and a
pig. How would you
have drawn this?

Close your eyes and doodle a cool cat.

IMAGINE YOU'RE A ZOOLOGIST.
WHAT WOULD YOU LOOK LIKE?

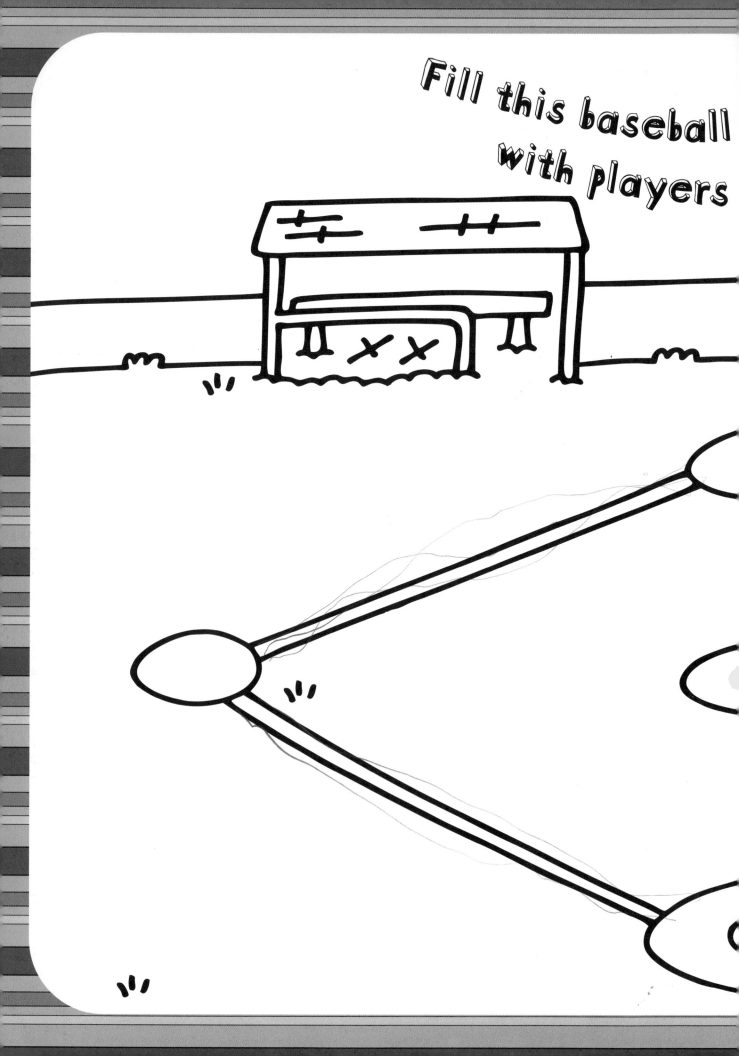

TURN THIS TRIANGLE INTO A CREATURE YOU MIGHT FIND IN THE WILD.

Doodle your favourite creature with big teeth.

Make all of these parrots look the same.

Our artist has drawn
a combination of a
monkey, a bear and a
butterfly. How would
you have drawn this?

FILL THIS COUNTRYSIDE SCENE WITH LOTS OF CREATURES YOU'D EXPECT TO SEE.

Use torn up pieces of magazines to create a summer scene.

FILL THIS RAINFOREST WITH THE ANIMALS YOU'D EXPECT TO SEE.

LOOK AT THE STEPS THAT THE ARTIST HAS GONE THROUGH TO DRAW A CARTOON KANGAROO. NOW DRAW YOUR OWN.

DRAW SOME MORE PENGUINS
TO KEEP THIS PENGUIN WARM.

Design your own mandala using the picture as an example.

SOME TREES ARE GROWN TO LOOK STRANGE.

DESIGN YOUR OWN STRANGE TREE.

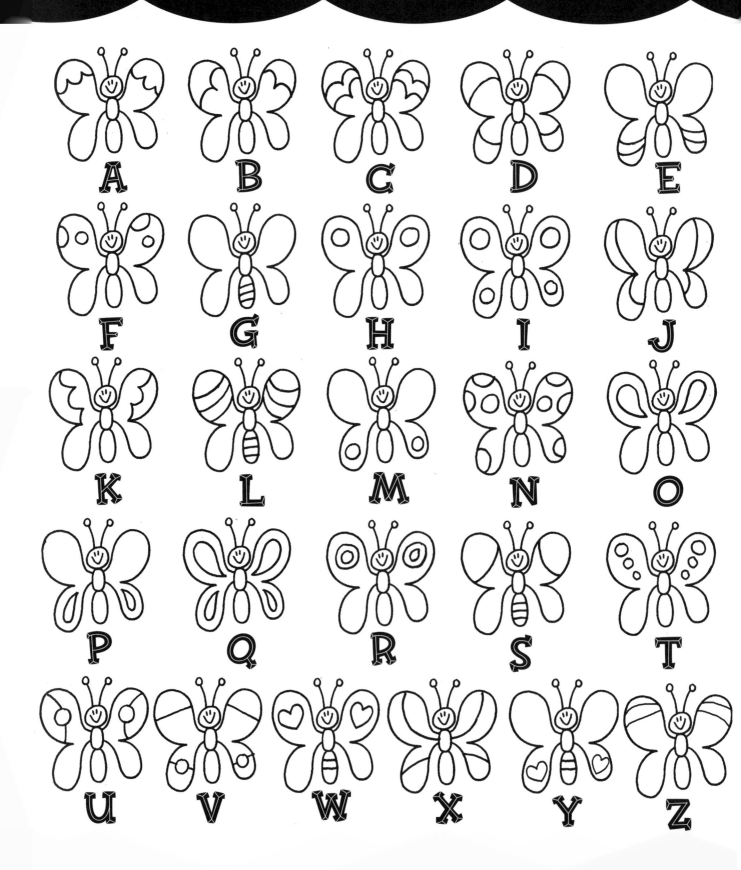

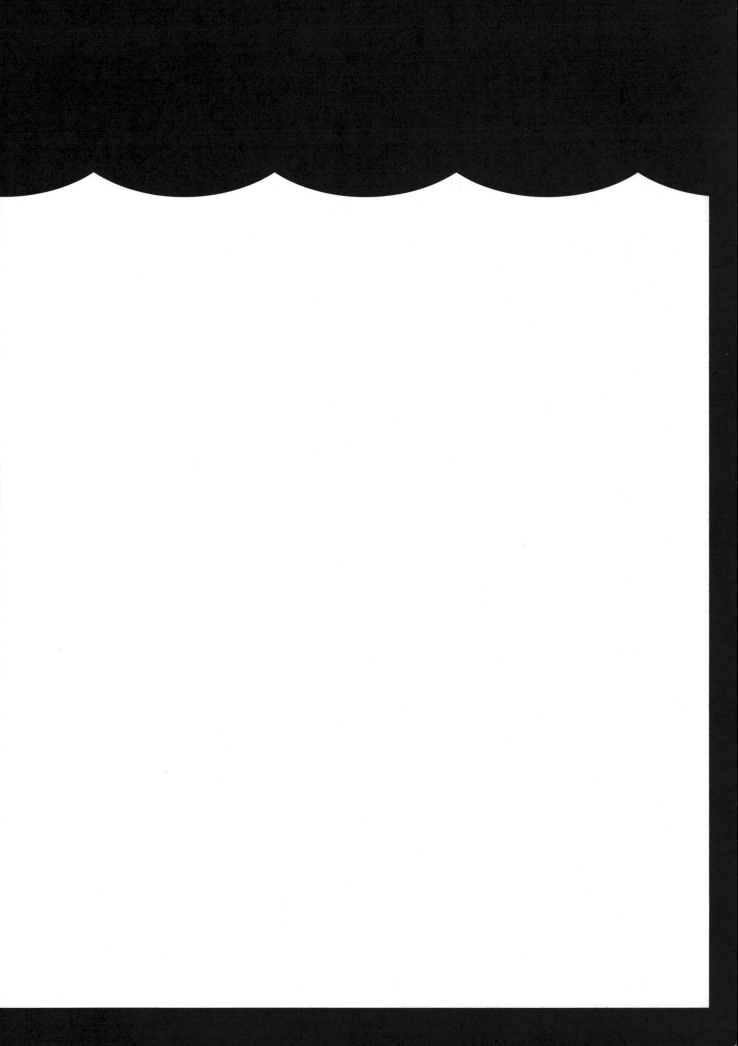

DRAW THIS OCTOPUS'S LEGS.

Mosaics

Complete this picture.

Dolphin's head

Cheetah's body

Zebra's legs

Design a new road sign for 'SHEEP CROSSING'.

WHAT IS HIDING BEHIND THIS ROCK?

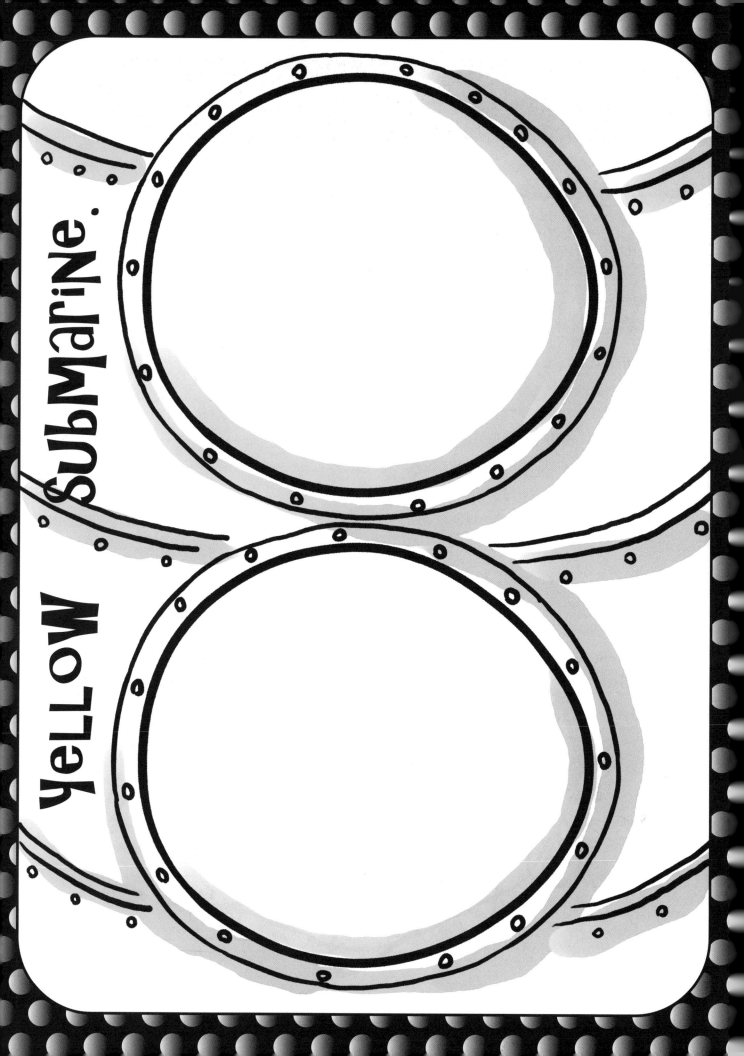

Yellow Submarine.

COMPLETE THE FISH PICTURES AND MAKE EACH FISH LOOK THE SAME AS THE FIRST.

PRETEND YOU LIVE IN A TREE HOUSE. WHAT DOES IT LOOK LIKE?

FILL THIS VASE WITH BEAUTIFUL FLOWERS.

Dip your fingers in some finger paint and make fingerprints on the page. When dry, turn them into different animals.

DRAW A GARDEN FOR THIS DOG TO PLAY IN.

Our artist has drawn
a combination of a
cockerel, a polar
bear and a sheep.
How would you have
drawn this?

DESiGN a NEW SPECiES OF FiSH.
WHat WOULD yOU Call it?

LOOK AT THE STEPS THAT THE ARTIST HAS GONE THROUGH TO DRAW A CARTOON DOG. NOW DRAW YOUR OWN.

What would a lion and a horse look like if they got mixed up?

Draw the squirrel that made this pile of nuts.

Design a new road sign for 'FLOODING'.

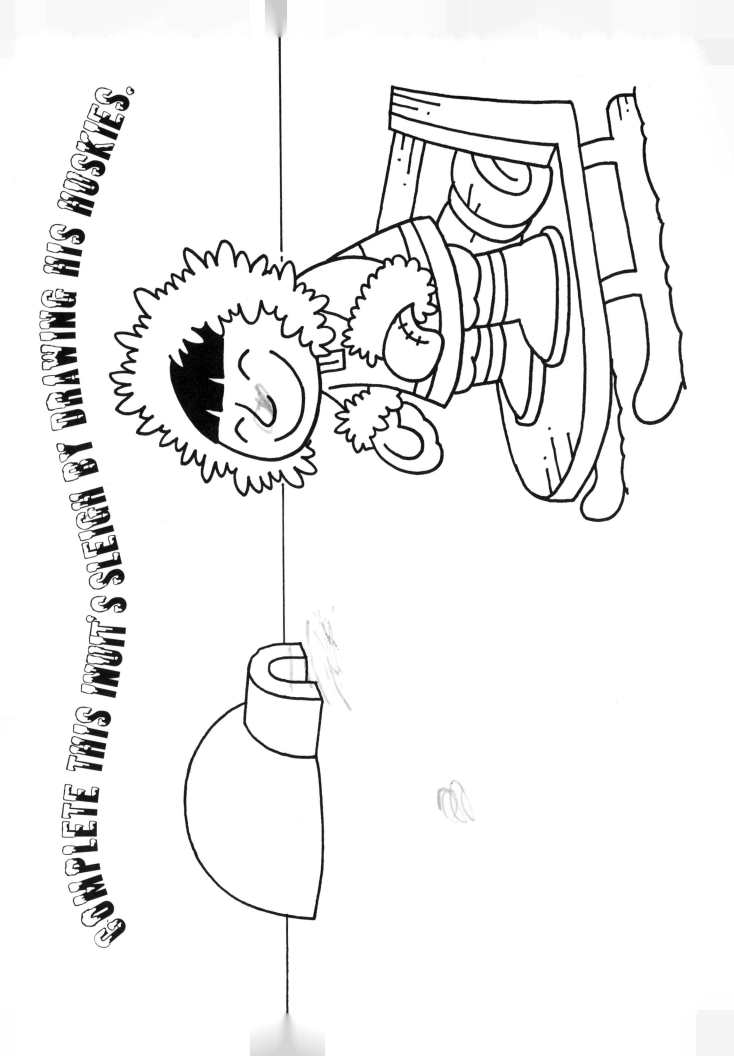

COMPLETE THIS INUIT'S SLEIGH BY DRAWING HIS HUSKIES.

Turn this rectangle into a plant or flower.

Can you turn
these leaf
shapes
into insects?

This picture has been started. Complete it any way you like.

Doodle your favourite thing with fins.

TIGER

Our artist has drawn
a combination of a
parrot, a sheep and
a horse. How would
you have drawn this?

PRETEND YOU LIVE AT THE BOTTOM OF THE OCEAN. WHAT DOES YOUR HOME LOOK LIKE?

Design a new road sign for 'AVALANCHE'.

IT'S RAINING CATS AND DOGS. WHAT DOES THIS LOOK LIKE?

What would a duck and a flamingo look like if they got mixed up?

IMAGINE YOU'RE OUT AT SEA.
WHAT DO YOU SEE IN THE SKY?

DRAW LOTS OF THIRSTY ELEPHANTS AROUND THIS WATERING HOLE.

Create a pattern that depicts creatures of the ocean.

DESIGN A NEW SPECIES OF PLANT.

Fill this pond with creatures you'd expect to see.

DRAW A
FARM FOR
THIS COCKEREL.

WHAT IS THIS ROCK CLIMBER THINKING RIGHT NOW?

Close your eyes and doodle a hairy, hungry spider.

Draw a jaguar hiding among the spots.

DRAW A TROPICAL ISLAND FOR THESE SUNBATHERS.

How many dogs does this woman own?

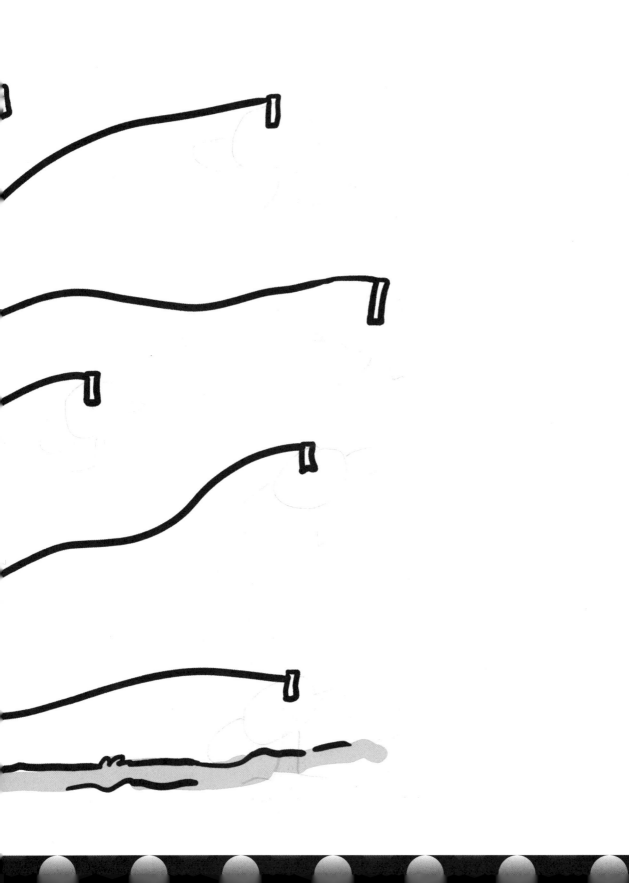

Find some unusually-shaped objects around your house and trace them. What sort of picture or pattern can you make?

GIVE THESE CREATURES WILD AND WACKY TAILS.

YOU'VE CAUGHT A MYSTERIOUS CREATURE ON CAMERA. DRAW IT ON THE PHOTOGRAPH.

IMagiNe you are a diver and you Make a discovery. WHat is it?

sea porcke Man

Trace your hand and turn it into a bird of paradise.

A
doodlebug
has crawled
over the page.
Turn the pattern
into a picture.

Make these iguanas look different.

Design a
new road sign for 'Warning! Bees'

WHO SAID WHAT? WRITE WHAT THESE CREATURES ARE SAYING TO EACH OTHER.

Trace your hand and turn it into a happy hedgehog.

DRAW A LADYBIRD FROM FOUR DIFFERENT ANGLES.

COMPLETE THIS WALLPAPER.

WheRe iS the BeeS' hiVe?

Our artist has drawn a combination of a ladybird, an ant and a grasshopper. How would you have drawn this?

Draw a frog without letting any lines cross.

Decorate this letter.

WHAT DO YOU THINK THIS IS AN EXTREME CLOSE UP OF? DRAW THE OBJECT BELOW.

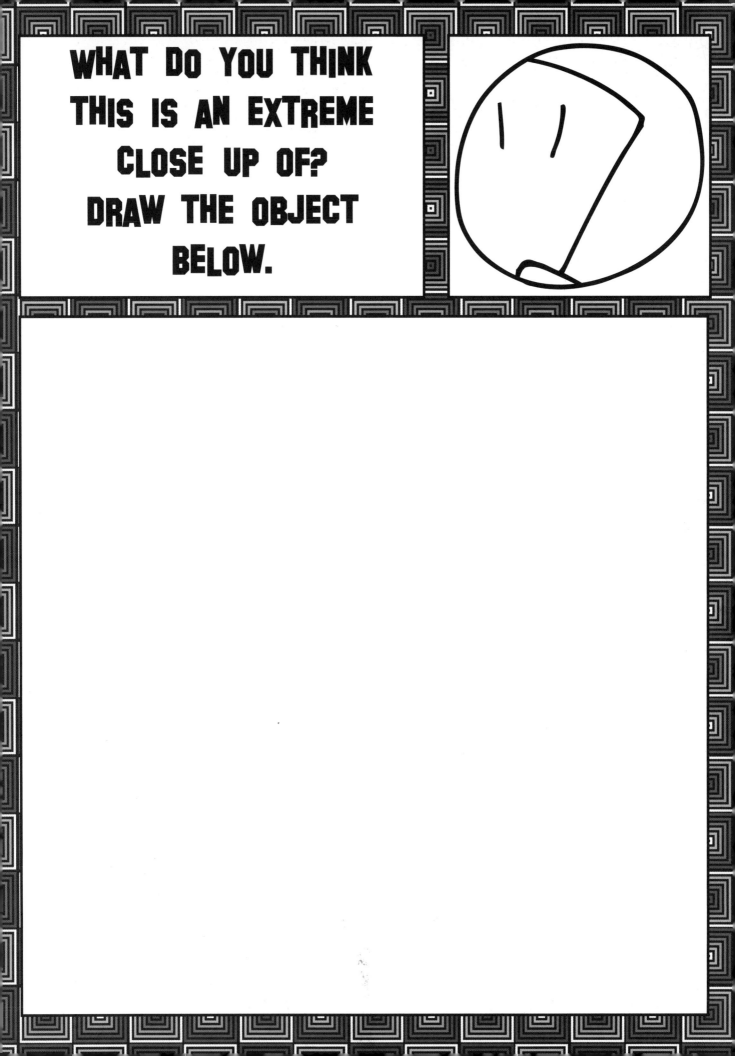

DOODLE YOUR FAVOURITE HAIRY BEAST.

Doodle an army of ants.

Using torn up pieces of magazine, use colours to create an autumn scene.

COLOUR THE GREEN WATERING CANS YELLOW, THE RED WATERING CAN BLUE, THE YELLOW WATERING CANS PURPLE AND THE BLUE WATERING CAN PINK.

A mysterious plant is growing in
your garden. Could it be dangerous?

LOOK AT THE STEPS THAT THE ARTIST HAS GONE THROUGH TO DRAW A CARTOON MOUSE. NOW DRAW YOUR OWN.

FILL THIS OCEAN WITH creatures you'd eXPeCt to See.

Create a pattern that is made from natural shapes (leaves, feathers, footprints etc).

Tear a sheet of paper into small pieces and drop them randomly onto your page. Trace each piece and make them into a rainforest scene.

MAKE THESE PEBBLES MORE INTERESTING.

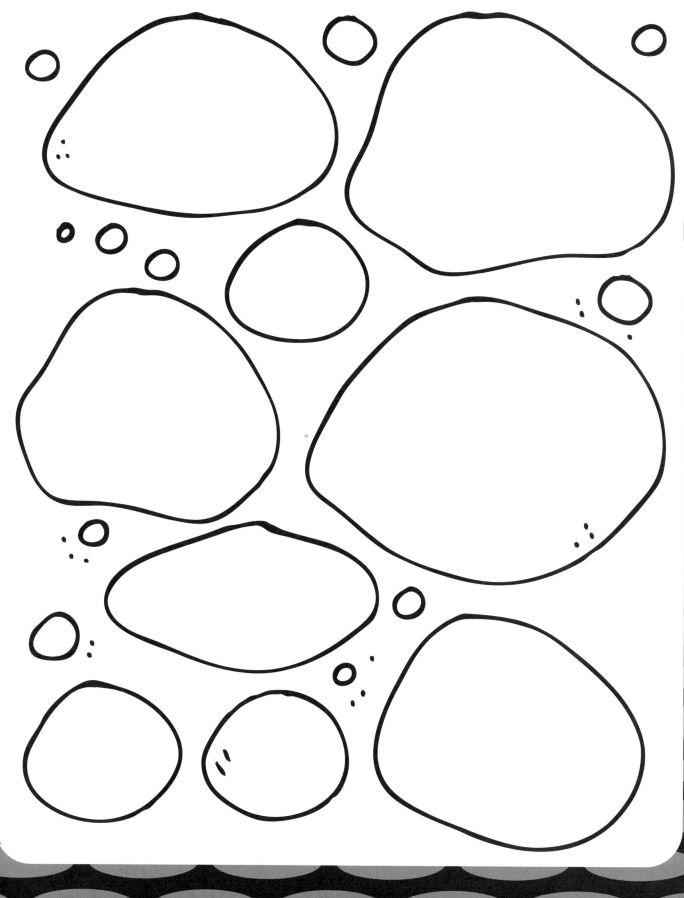

Give these creatures colourful shells for their fashion parade!

Draw what you think a doodlebug looks like. What does it eat?

Quick! The dinosaur is wreaking havoc on the town. Design a way to stop it.

Draw more blocks. What shape will you make them into?

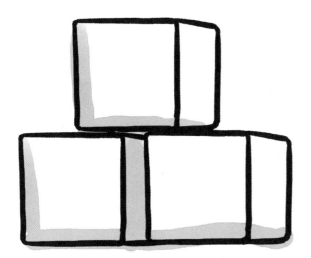

Draw a picture of a person without lifting your pencil from the paper.

Design a poster for the new up-and-coming film 'PENGUINS IN THE CITY'.

Complete this maze.
Draw what you see on the way.

WHAT HAS SCARED THE FISH AND THE DIVER AWAY?

Who said what? Write what these people are saying to each other.

DRAW HOW MANY THINGS YOU CAN THINK OF THAT BEGIN WITH THE LETTER L.

CAN YOU TURN THIS PICTURE OF A PENCIL INTO SOMETHING ELSE?

Give this lion an impressive mane.
Now draw him in the savannah with his pride.

USE THESE FLOWERS AS EYES AND CREATE A FACE BY DRAWING THINGS YOU FIND IN THE GARDEN.

WHAT DO YOU THINK THIS IS AN EXTREME CLOSE UP OF? DRAW THE OBJECT BELOW.

Draw a cheetah among the spots.

Trace your hand and turn it into an exotic bug-eating plant.

INVENT SOMETHING MORE EFFECTIVE THAN AN UMBRELLA TO STOP YOU FROM GETTING WET IN THE RAIN.

DOODLE A TROOP OF BABOONS.

What would a tiger and a crocodile look like if they got mixed up?

USE TORN UP PIECES OF MAGAZINE
TO CREATE A WINTER SCENE.

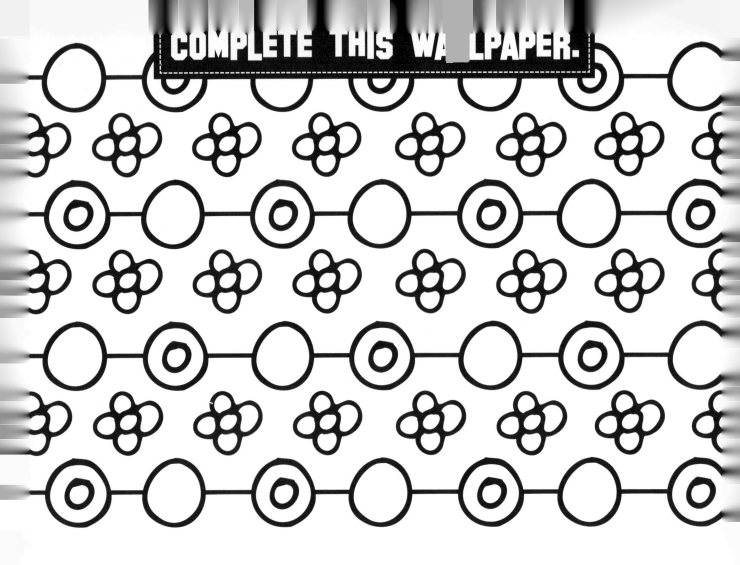

COMPLETE THIS WA LPAPER.

DRAW AN OCEAN SCENE AND SEA LIFE
FOR THESE DIVERS.

Create a jungle gymnasium
to help animals keep fit!

GIVE THESE BIRDS WILD AND WACKY TAILS.

What has this photographer taken a picture of?

GIVE THIS POND SOME DUCKS.

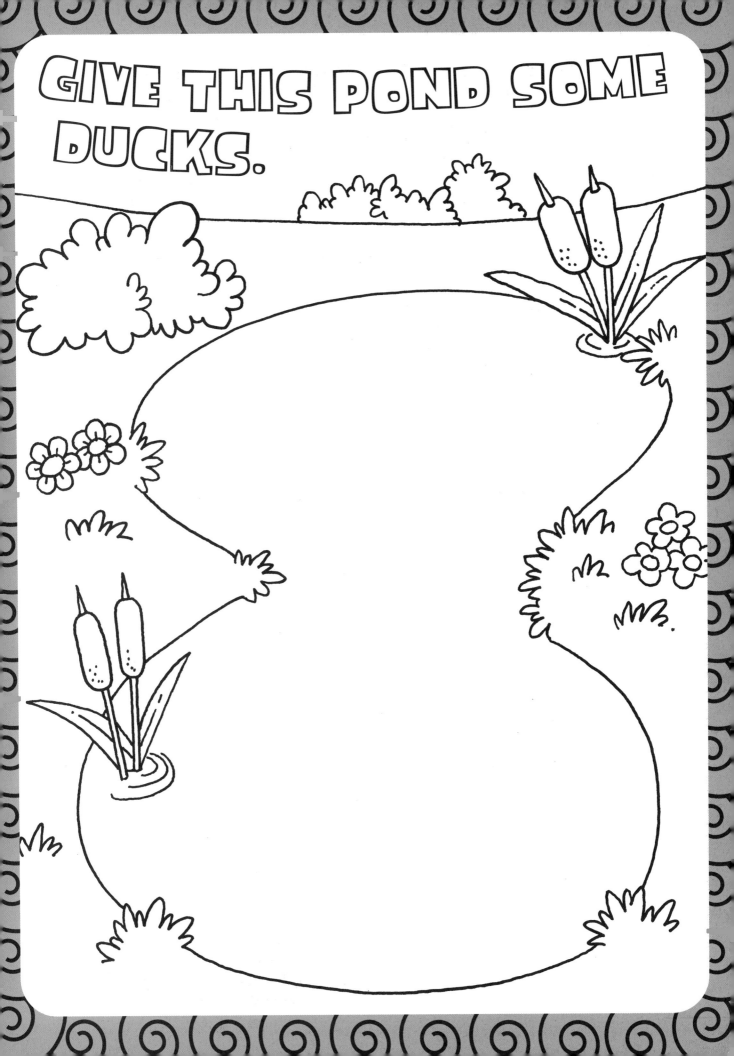

PIPES RUN UNDERNEATH ALL MAJOR CITIES. COMPLETE THIS NETWORK OF PIPES. WHAT CREATURES CAN YOU SEE LURKING AROUND?

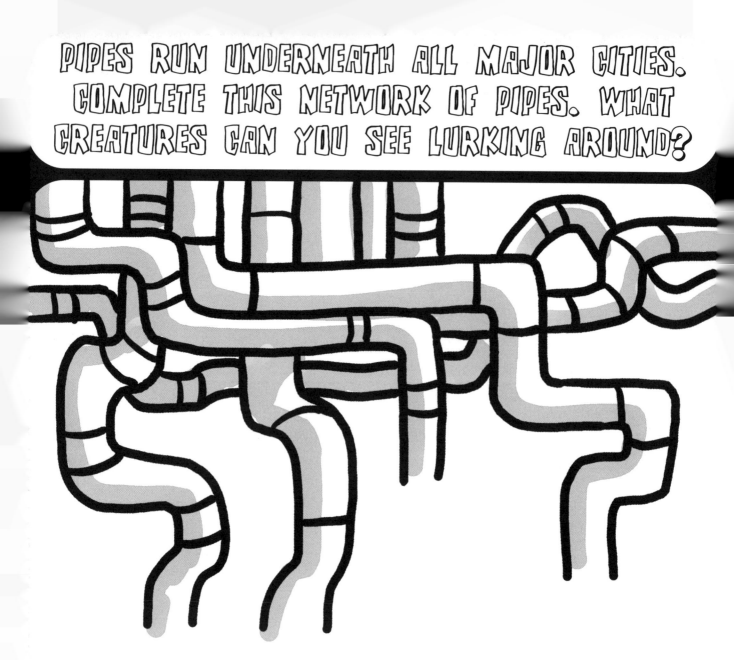

Trace around your hand and use your imagination to create a newly-discovered animal.

ALL at Sea!

EAGER BEAVER.

Doodle your favourite mini bug.

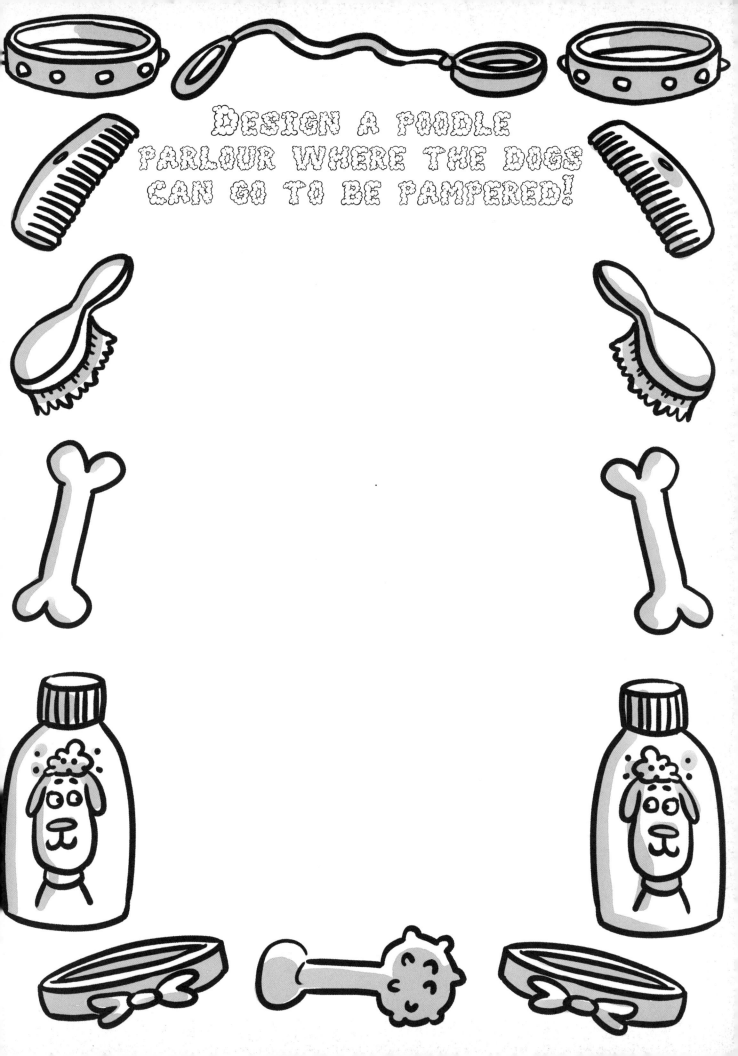

DESIGN A POODLE
PARLOUR WHERE THE DOGS
CAN GO TO BE PAMPERED!

GIVE THESE LEMONS FUNNY FACES.

DRAW HOW
YOU THINK YOUR
TOWN WOULD
LOOK FROM A
BIRD'S
PERSPECTIVE.

DRAW THE PETS YOU THINK THESE PEOPLE WOULD OWN.

Try to draw this ladybird with the hand you don't normally write with. It's not as easy as it looks!

Give these trowels and forks
brightly-coloured handles.

Draw different patterns on these snakes.

LOOK AT THE STEPS THAT THE ARTIST HAS GONE THROUGH TO DRAW A CARTOON CAT. NOW DRAW YOUR OWN.

WHAT IS THE ELEPHANT SCARED OF?

What would a panda and a pig look like if they got mixed up?

Scribbling can be a lot of fun.
Cover this page with random scribbles and doodles.

Give this cat a comfy place to sleep.

THIS EXPLORER IS LOOKING FOR BUTTERFLIES. HOW MANY CAN YOU SPOT? DRAW SOME MORE.

Doodle a gaggle of geese.

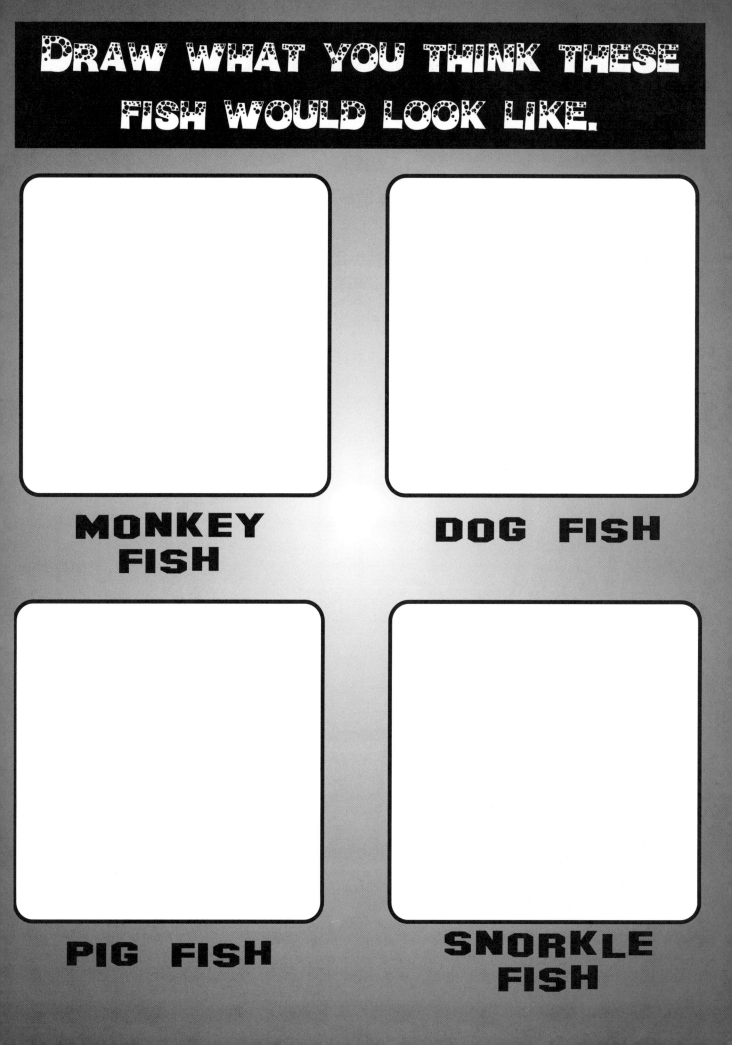

WHAT'S HAPPENING OUTSIDE OF THIS CITY HALL?

IMAGINE YOU ARE AN
EXPLORER IN THE
DEEPEST JUNGLE.
WHAT NEW
SPECIES OF ANIMAL
HAVE YOU
DISCOVERED?

LOOK AT A LEAF UNDER A MAGNIFYING GLASS.

DRAW WHAT YOU SEE.

Collect some interesting stones, twigs, leaves and fallen petals from your garden or a park. Trace them on the page to create an interesting scene.

YOU HAVE DISCOVERED A NEW TYPE OF FLOWER. DRAW IT IN THE BOX AND DESCRIBE IT ON THE LINES. WHAT IS IT CALLED? IS IT POISONOUS? DOES IT SMELL?

_____

_____

_____

_____

Draw a playground and some children.

Our artist has drawn a combination of a snake, a horse and a pig. How would you have drawn this?

DOODLE A LITTER OF KITTENS.

DRAW DIFFERENT PATTERNS ON THESE DOGS' COATS.

What would an ostrich and a giraffe look like if they got mixed up?

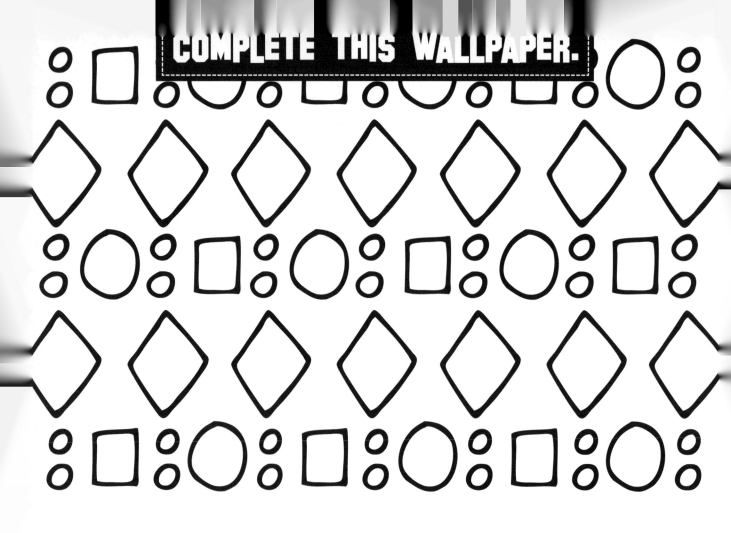

COMPLETE THIS WALLPAPER.

DRAW THE CREATURE THAT HAS MADE THESE FOOTPRINTS.

Draw some animals in this

savannah scene.

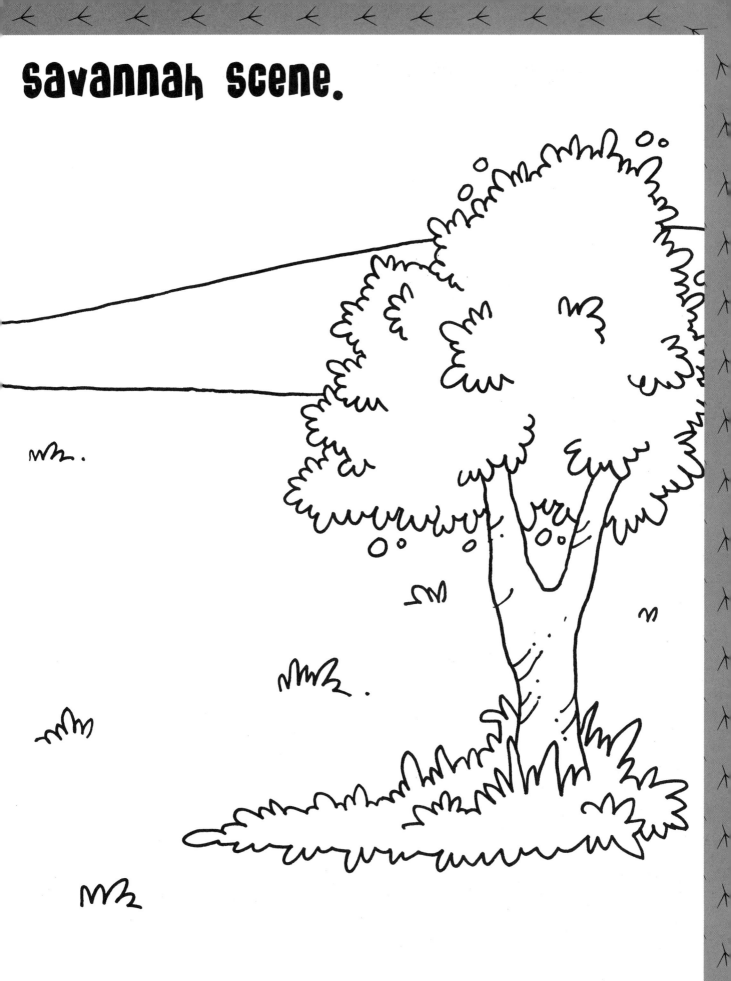

Help each lizard to hide by providing camouflage

to match its surroundings.

WHAT DO YOU THINK THIS IS AN EXTREME CLOSE UP OF? DRAW THE OBJECT BELOW.

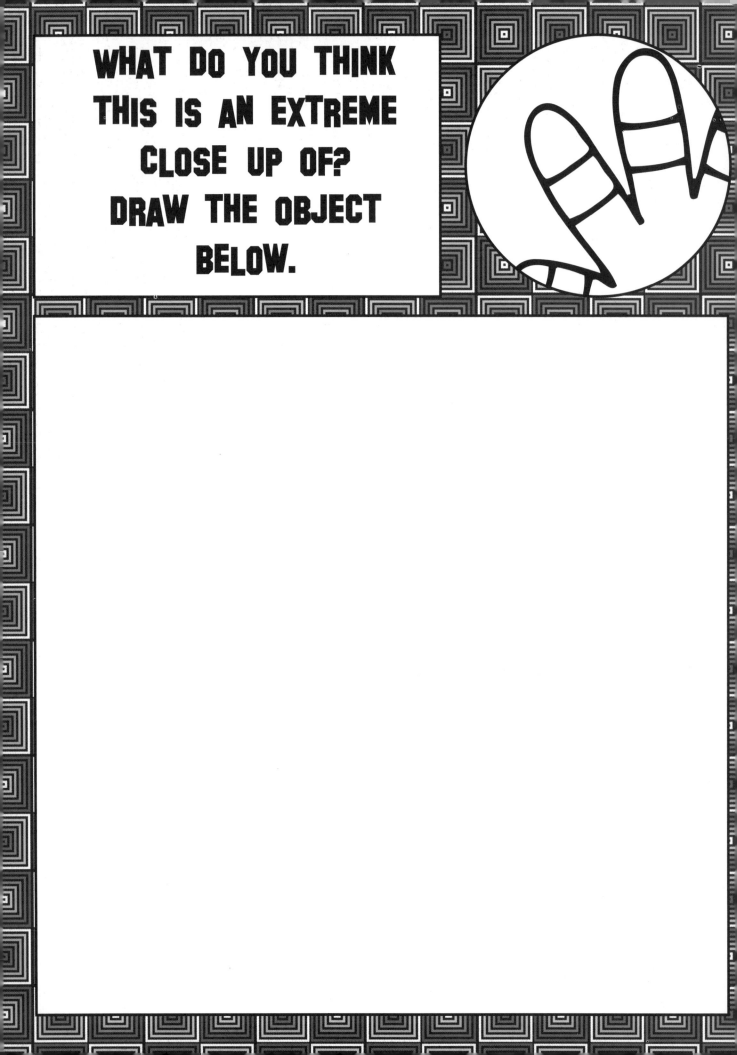

Close your eyes and draw this bird.
It's not easy!

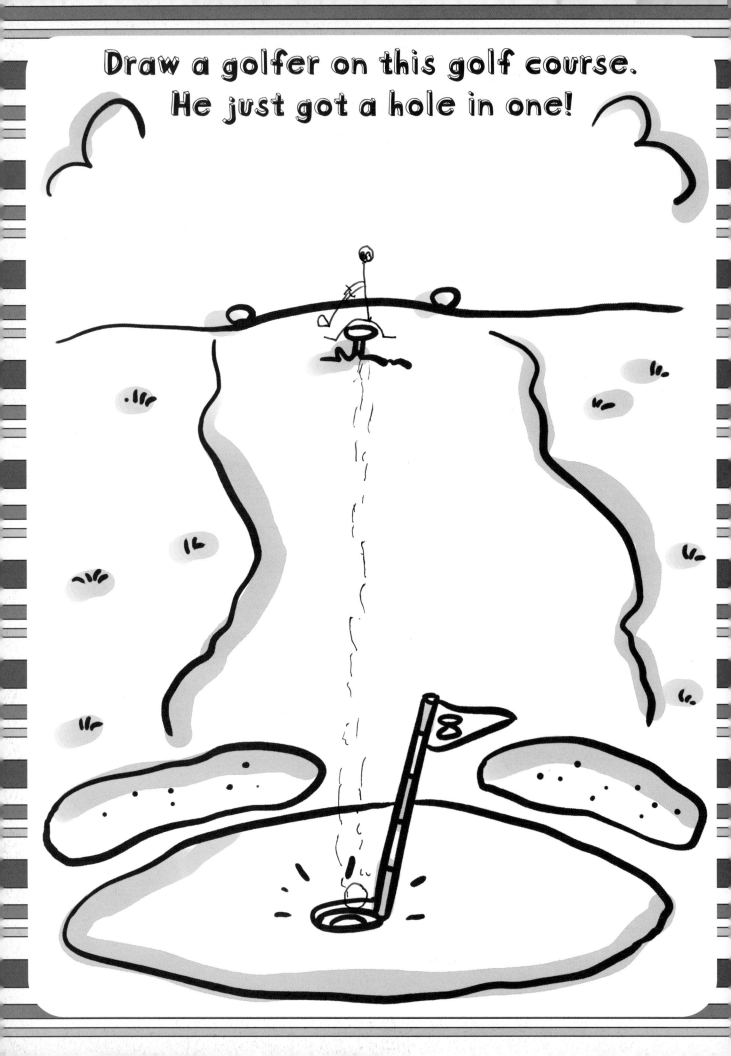

What sort of creatures can you make out of these shapes?

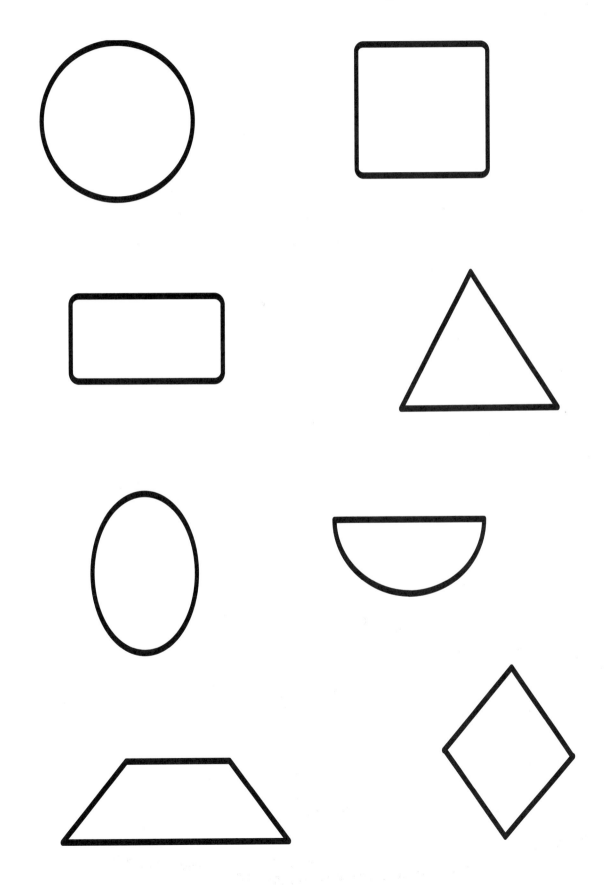

Mosaics

DRAW A KENNEL SO THIS DOG CAN HIDE FROM THE RAIN.

Turn this island into a tropical paradise with lots of plants and flowers.

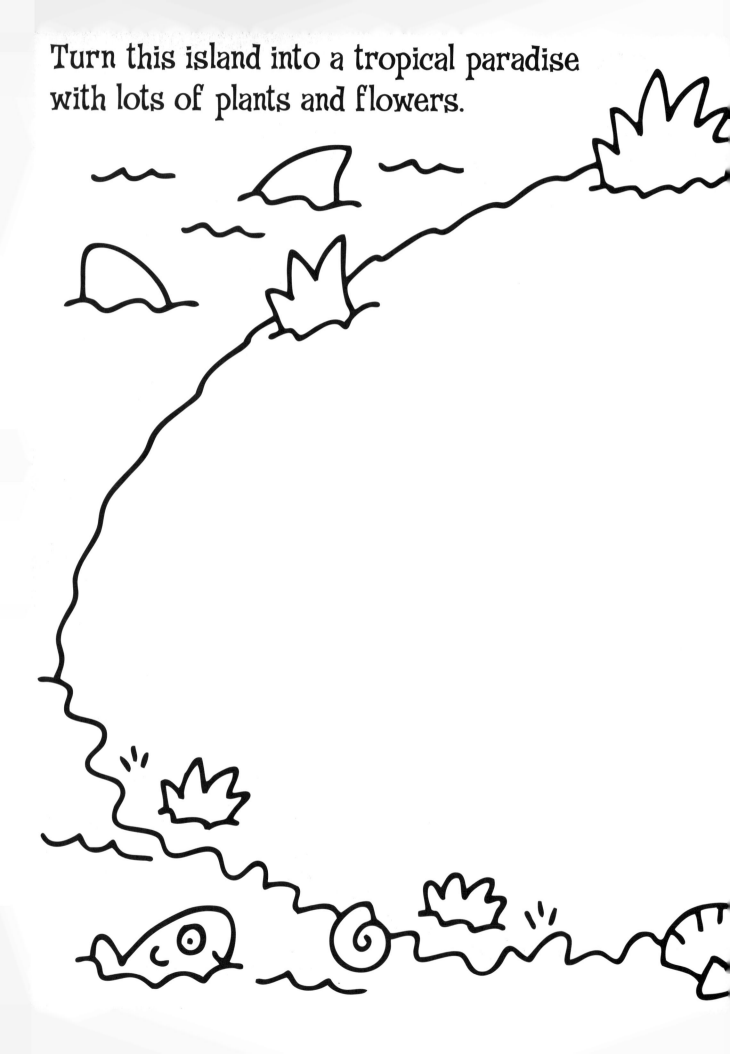

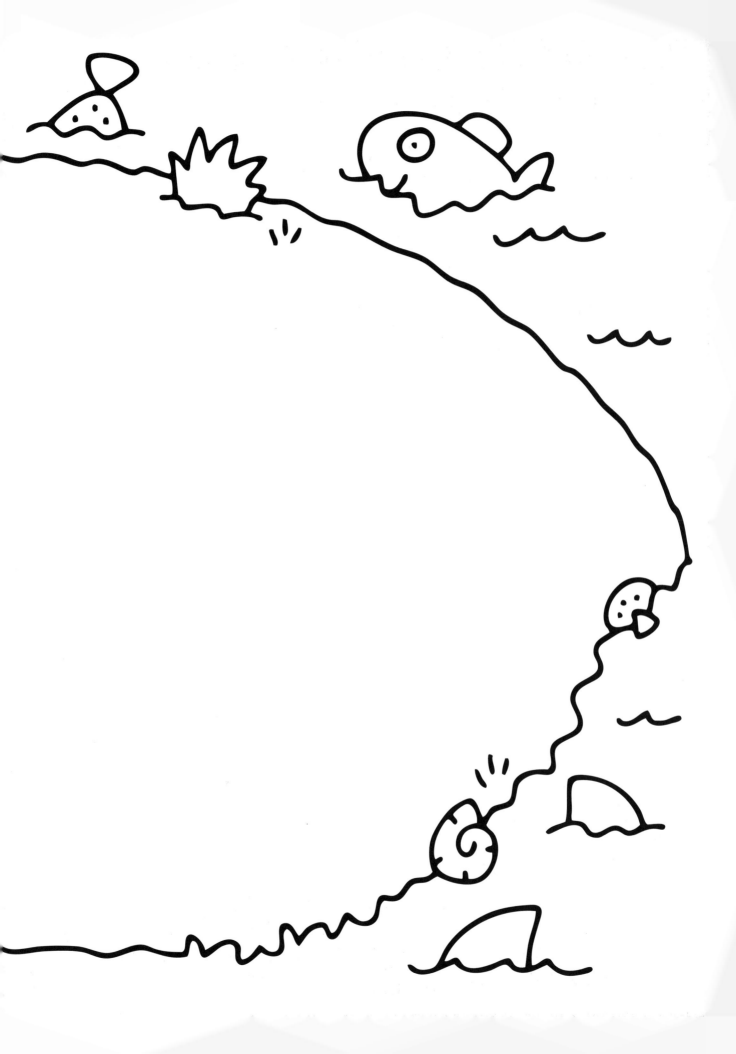

DRAW A PAGE OF SNOWFLAKES. MAKE SURE EACH ONE IS DIFFERENT.

Close your eyes and doodle a crocodile at the dentist.

HOW MANY THINGS CAN YOU THINK OF THAT BEGIN WITH THE LETTER G? DRAW THEM.

DRAW SOME THINGS YOU WOULDN'T EXPECT TO SEE GROWING ON A TREE. ONE'S BEEN DONE FOR YOU!

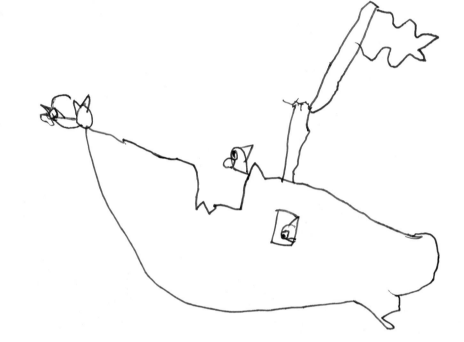

Draw how you think your room would look from an ant's perspective.

What would a penguin and a beaver look like if they got mixed up?

Draw a giraffe among the spots.

DRAW THE BIRD THAT LIVES IN THIS NEST.

Complete this picture.

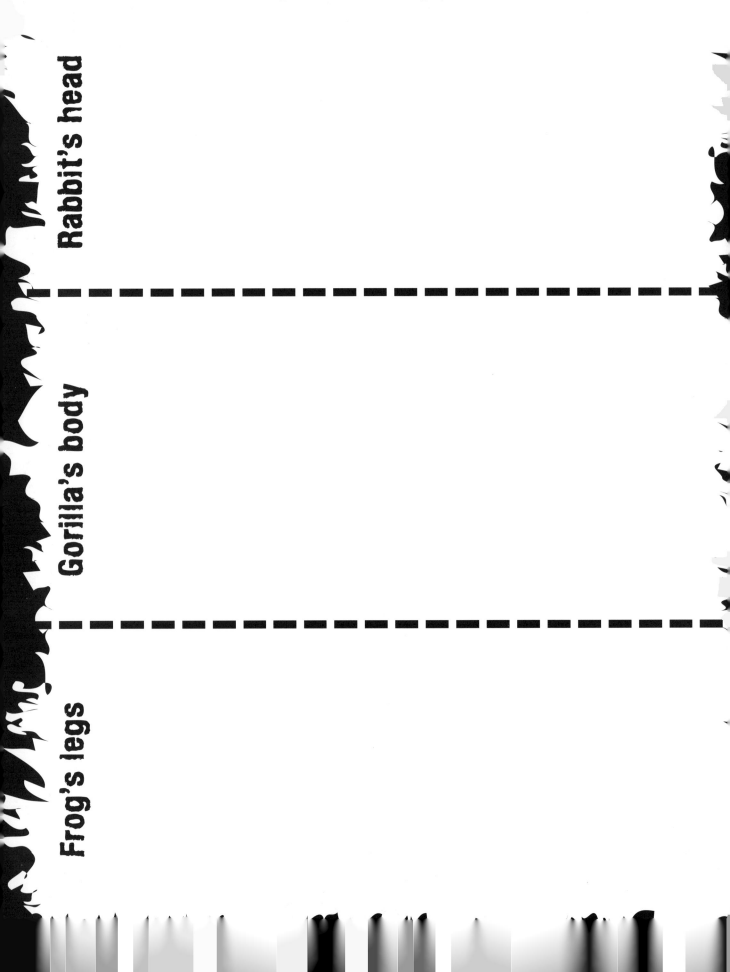

Rabbit's head

Gorilla's body

Frog's legs

Draw a scene showing spring transforming into winter.

Mosaics

Our artist has drawn a combination of an elephant, a zebra and a whale. How would you have drawn this?

Turn this circle into something you see outside.

Doodle your favourite
creature that
hangs around in trees.

DESIGN YOUR OWN T-SHIRT.
WHERE WOULD YOU WEAR IT?

Draw a zebra
among the stripes.

CREATE A NEW SPECIES OF dinosaur.

Draw a picture of a dog without lifting your pencil from the paper.

Trace your hand onto the centre of the page and turn it into a butterfly.

WHAT'S BEHIND HIM?

Imagine you are a cat.
What would you draw?

Complete this filmstrip.

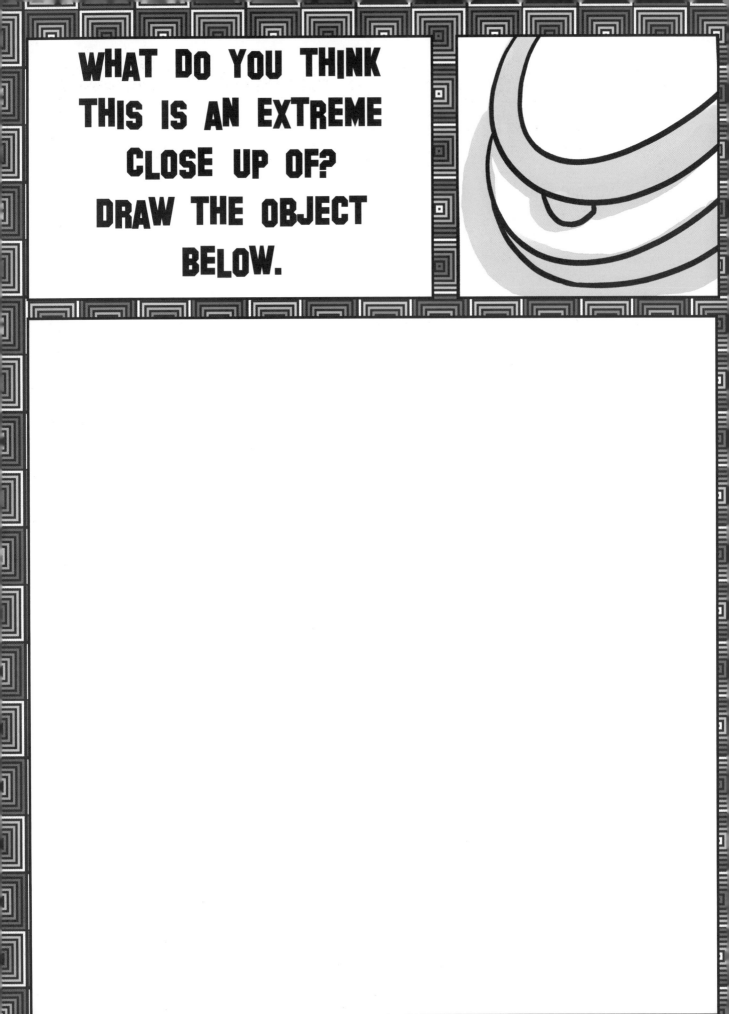

WHAT DO YOU THINK THIS IS AN EXTREME CLOSE UP OF? DRAW THE OBJECT BELOW.

Try to draw this dog with the hand you don't normally write with. It's not as easy as it looks!

FILL THiS UNDerWater SCeNe WiTH

What you'd expect to see.

WHO IS ON SAFARI?

WHAT HAS THIS GIANT SPIDER CAUGHT IN HIS WEB?

Doodle your favourite jungle animal.

Our artist has drawn
a combination
of a cat, a dog
and a hamster.
How would you have drawn this?

Use these pages to just doodle. You can do as many as you like, the only rule is that they must not touch, overlap or interfere with each other.

When you have finished, colour it in.

Our artist has drawn
a combination
of a kangaroo,
a dolphin and
a crab.
How would you have drawn this?